Outside the Gates of Eden

OUTSIDE THE GATES OF EDEN

Poems by

David Middleton

Measure Press
Savannah, Georgia

The text of this book is composed in Baskerville.
Composition by R.G.
Manufacturing by Ingram.

Middleton, David
  Outside the Gates of Eden / by David Middleton — 1st ed.

  ISBN-13: 978-1-939574-34-3
  ISBN-10: 1-939574-34-X
  Library of Congress Control Number: 2023941718

Cover art: "North Louisiana Field in Autumn" (1972) by David V. Middleton, Jr. (1922-1996), oil on panel.

Cover art photograph by Deborah Lillie, Department of Art, Nicholls State University, Thibodaux, Louisiana.

Photograph of David Middleton by Misty McElroy, Photojournalist, Nicholls State University, Thibodaux, Louisiana.

Frontispiece: "Old Broken Gate" by David V. Middleton, Jr. (1922-1996), pen and ink.

Measure Press
2 Longberry Lane
Savannah, GA 31419
http://www.measurepress.com/measure/

Acknowledgments

Poems in this collection first appeared, sometimes in earlier versions, in the following publications:

As Far As Light Remains (The Cummington Press, 1993)
The Abbeville Review
Alabama Literary Review
The Anglican: A Quarterly Journal of Anglican Identity
The Anglican Theological Review
Chronicles: A Magazine of American Culture
The Classical Outlook
The Evansville Review
First Things
Jambalaya Writers Conference Anthology (2011, 2014, 2015, 2017 issues)
The Language of the Heart (Louisiana Literature Press, Poetry Chapbook 4, 2003)
Louisiana Literature
Measure: A Review of Formal Poetry
Modern Age: A Quarterly Review
North American Anglican
The Sewanee Review
The Southern Review

I wish to express my gratitude for, and admiration of, R. V. Young — editor, scholar, critic, and fellow poet — who defends "the permanent things."

for
Francine Anne Kerne Middleton
artist, scholar, wife, companion, friend

And the Lord God planted a garden eastward in Eden; and there he put the man whom he had formed.

— *Genesis* 2:8

Som natural tears they drop'd, but wip'd them soon;
The World was all before them, where to choose
Thir place of rest, and Providence thir guide:
They hand in hand with wandring steps and slow,
Through *Eden* took thir solitarie way.

— John Milton, *Paradise Lost*, Book XII

I want to go to the Garden of Eden.

— Dylan Thomas, near death

We are still in Eden; the wall that shuts us out of the garden is our own ignorance and folly.

— Thomas Cole, "Essay on American Scenery" (1836)

And there are no truths outside the gates of Eden.

— Bob Dylan, "Gates of Eden"

CONTENTS

Outside the Gates of Eden

Night Watchman at the Zoo

Audubon Zoo, New Orleans, Louisiana

The day's last visitors have left the zoo
Taking the golden autumn afternoon
Along with gift shop toys their children hug —
Stuffed lions smiling wide, soft cuddly bears,
Limber rubber snakes showing rubber fangs,
A windup ape beating its plastic chest —
All headed home to nightlights, bed, and prayers.

And here, as gates lock shut when sunset flames,
My flashlight, cell phone, pistol close at hand,
I walk the narrow pathways as they fade
Between these artificial habitats —
Savannahs, caves, pools, jungles, waterfalls —
A wilderness constrained by moat and bar,
A red wolf kept from swamp hares by the wire,
A cheetah's caged eyes fixed on still gazelles.

By each exhibit, tilted on a post,
An illustrated plate states what we know
Of origin and range, defining traits,
The bony abstract Latin, English flesh,
Cemophora coccinea, scarlet snake,
Zoologist and poet nearly one.

I watch for quiet intruders who provide
Stolen calves and cubs to the roadside zoos
Where they will languish, maddened in their cells,
Or offer them as curios to those
So rich and bored they need menageries,
Pure spectacle, a conversation piece.

But I'm on guard to thwart them as the heir
Of Adam who tamed animals with names,
Addressing them in ur-speech, early words,
The owl's prime Eden screech for colloquy.

Such animals still speak, their language maimed
As hisses, hoots, growls, bays we try to learn
As some of them can learn our blunt commands
Though most live in a state beyond recall,
Detecting with their feelers, bristles, tongues
A lessened world by appetite confined.

They're fed enough to keep them satisfied,
Their habitats shrunken to this small space,
Too captive-bred ever to hunt again.

I hear them eating far into the dark,
So seemingly at peace with humankind
That knows them as they cannot know themselves.

And yet I often think of Trajan's games,
Massed gladiators spearing crocodiles,
Or Nero's where starved tigers slaughtered bulls
As bulls did tigers, hundreds at a time
And how in our own day we still permit
Chinese safari parks where those who come
Pay to toss goats alive to waiting lions
Who kill and eat, feeding a savage glee.

Such images disturb me as I move
Between flamingos swirling water-stars,
Walking with grace through pools while overhead
Old houses with their Lion, Serpent, Bears
Mark gardens walled from floods the heavens hold,
Flaring against a ground no word declares.

Soon dawn will hide the stars-beasts in its light
And visitors will gather at the booths
Eager to walk the daytime's crowded paths
Till I, like Adam, waking from his sleep,
Return to watch the night out once again
While dreaming children clutch their gift shop toys,
Loved animals they hug and kiss by name
So far from Michael's sword and that first sin
Which drove us out of Eden to a place
Where closing gates lock shut as sunset flames.

Before and After Sleep

Late afternoon. Then twilight. Then the night
When nightmare-sleep and sleeplessness contend.
No Lethe-drop to drink. A heart not right
With what the mind alone would comprehend:

The first and final question, where we go
And where we come from, why we sojourn here,
The Big Bang and Big Rip the bounds we know
Around these flat-earth plains of *mere* and *sheer*.

Yet from some prime elusive shadow-seed —
Its physics welling in the seen-unseen —
Unfold proportions noble in their breed,
The Golden Numbers and the Golden Mean:

The spiraling florets of flower heads,
The curve of shell and beak, of horn and claw,
The whirling squares a logarithm spreads
Through everything by Fibonacci's law,

Or Pegasus, whom Ptolemy could trace
In radiant matrices — the fountain's sheen —
Descending star by star through time and space
Till hooves struck rock and freed the Hippocrene.

Alabama Correspondences:
Winter into Spring

1
Flowers Hospital, Dothan

2/17/91

Somewhere in Flowers,
Some antiseptic room,
Too weak to keep on breathing
You finally died of AIDS
This first Lenten Sunday
My old poet-friend
Of almost twenty years.
Miles west, near Enterprise,
Across the family farm
Through quiet trees outside
The house you thought and wrote in
A sinking wind still cries.

2
Huntsville

2/18/91

Unable to deny
Her bonding-place and time,
She turns at last and comes
To one whose early poems
Some twenty years ago
Had touched her being's core.
Tired of some blank sadness,
The sterilized tight void
Where joy's wildflowers should bloom,
She writes him from her room.
Her words like daisies blaze
Brightening more and more.

Woman Mending

after the drawing by Jean-François Millet (1814-1875)
1853
black conté crayon on blue-gray paper
private collection, London

So inward and so near to us the scene
We fear we are intruding just to look
At one intent, yet patient and serene,
Giving herself to work that must be done.

Her practiced fingers, bent, adroitly poised
To use a pitted thimble, needle tip
Pull tight the thread that stitches closed a hole
In a woolen shirt, rumpled in her lap.

A shelf holds piled-up clothes still unrepaired
In the dim, bare room. Scissors hang in reach
From her chair's left stile, ribbon looped through rings,
Blades hidden by her sewing basket's weave.

Such mending never seems to have an end —
The ready fingers, things unraveling . . .
Yet passing through a window just unseen
Light rests like grace and fate on thread and hand.

Arcadian Shepherds

after the painting by Nicolas Poussin (1594-1665)
oil and canvas, 1639

> *You cannot take your song with you*
> *In the end. Hades and forgetfulness are the same.*
> — Theocritus, *Idyll 1, The Passion of Daphnis*
> (translation by Robert Wells)

They happen on a tomb on which no name
Has been inscribed, three shepherds without flocks
Or panpipes, although two of them are wreathed,
For death and art have come to Arcady.

Behind them, straight or leaning, peaks and trees
Seem sentient attendants waiting near.
Low slate and high white cloud-shapes pass and stay
Under a shading sky's cerulean blue.

There, too, a woman, or a goddess, stands,
Her left wrist on her hip, her right hand placed
Upon one shepherd's back, knowledge and calm
Acceptance in her pale gray-yellow face.

The shepherd whom she comforts turns his head
While pointing at block capitals — shocked eyes
Searching the fixed placidity of hers
That look both deep within and far away.

Another shepherd rests against the tomb,
Brooding over a missing chunk of stone,
Still trying to interpret cryptic words:
ET IN ARCADIA EGO — nothing more.

The unwreathed shepherd, bearded, kneels to read,
By sight and touch, each character incised,
His finger tracing a shadow of itself,
Spelling his fate in lettered silhouette.

Who carved this verse, unfinished — without verb?
What mysteries of author, speaker, tense?
Who made this tomb where tombs had never been?
What master practiced here the arts of death?

It was and is Poussin, who, till the end,
Still painted, though with tremors in his hand,
The silence of his Stoic dignity
Like that of her who dominates the scene:

The mother of the Muses — Memory —
Whose shepherds drove their flocks toward piping cries
When Daphnis as a baby lay exposed,
Abandoned in a grove of laurel trees.

The Potter's Epitaph

Inside an urn my strong hands made
Those hands are in their ashes laid,
And I who quickened mother earth
Lie still within the place of birth.

New clay dug up from ancient pools
And fashioned by the timeless rules
Became a pot, conceived, then thrown
Till blended use and beauty shone.

And while it dried I took a knife
To cut blunt words of death and life
In verse that followed, sharply curved,
The potter's field I ruled and served.

Then when the last cone melting fell
In fires of Pentecost and Hell,
The hardened glazes baked and blazed
Black rhymes at which the kiln-gods gazed . . .

"Made both to hide and to expose
My burning flesh in cold repose,
This urn mocks all dark acts of birth,
Holding and yet held by earth."

Charts

Saline, Louisiana, 1957-1959

When I consider thy heavens, the work of thy fingers, the moon and the stars,
  which thou hast ordained,
What is man that thou art mindful of him?
            — Psalm 8:3-4

And there shall be signs in the sun, and in the moon, and in the stars . . .
            — Luke 21:25

in memory of my maternal grandfather, Henderson Edward Sudduth,
  1891-1959

1

You woke just as the sun and moon and stars,
Poised in their constant moving, blended lights,
A moment's single beam in dark and dawn
Spreading along the dense midwinter clouds,
Snow holding till it fell straight down like rain,
Dry shadow-drops in patterns on your bed.

Now sixty-five, finding it harder to rise
For one more day as village banker, mayor,
Church elder, still you did what must be done
Because your word, once given, was for good,
In oath and vow, in pledging the full tithe,
Plighting your troth in civic, private life,
And first to her beside you, dreaming on,
Emma your wife of over forty years.

You felt achy and stiff as you sat up,
Leaving the warmth of quilt and comforter,
Legs swinging till your feet touched cold wood floor,
That metal plate like weather in your head.

Unsteady, you shuffled along, room to room,
Turning up each gas heater's pilot light
Or scratching kitchen matches till a flame
Spread port to port behind the radiant grates.

But as you leaned toward burners in the hall,
Your right side deadened, nerves blocked off from brain —
That path between the muscles and the will —
Then you collapsed, half-paralyzed by stroke,
Those sounds that come before and after speech
Rousing a wife untroubled in her sleep
Who found you staring helpless past her eyes.

2

An ambulance soon there from Natchitoches,
Men pushed you on a gurney through the yard,
Immobilized by straps, your mind adrift,
Mixed flocks of birds and leaves on bough and ground,
Your body dotted with crystal hexagons.

And as red flashing sirens cleared the way
Past logging trucks loaded with sand-hill pine —
Their chain-links stressed and strained by dip and crest —
You slipped into another place and time
When medics with a stretcher reached your plane
Shot up by German gunners, limping back
With leaking gas aflame along the wings,
Gliding toward No Man's Land, topographies
Of ink and earth mapped out, their legends read,
The shock of sign and thing at odds and one.

You lived, but with a steel brace in your brow,
The hole in your right cheek a dimple-scar,
Those wounds the medals you would always wear.

Yet now, a harder fall, and you lay still,
Doctors scanning a clipboard by your bed,
Zigzagging needle peak and valley lines,
The heart's cartography, a brain surveyed.

In time you walked, foot-sliding on a cane,
Reason intact but speech a slur of words
Like a toddler's mangled language, though you strove
To grapple back through babble toward a voice
Eluding you ever after, damage done.

3

To let you say what needed to be said
As statement, question, answer, or request,
Your son-in-law, my father, drew a chart
On plywood — a rectangle painted white —
A straight row of numbers, zero to nine,
And two rows curving for the alphabet,
Then underneath YES, NO, HELLO, GOODBYE,
All taken from a talking board, and HELP,
Words ready if you grew too weak to spell.

And so you stayed, with silent dignity,
Hobbling in pain and numbness on the porch,
Your cane-tip tapping out its open code
Between the swing and rocker where you watched
For hours seeing more deeply than before:
Split husks dropping pecans through torn cocoons,
Strung stars and wrens along the winter limbs,
Spring lizards on the warming summer walls,
Sunflowers climbing noons toward noonday sun,
The grains they came from shaken from their heads.

And though at last bedridden, you held on,

Your sleep a kind of waking, waking, sleep,
Mind all but done with measuring the world —
God's copybook of tablet-clay and light —
Prefiguring equations, slated sums,
The ABCs that count the telling names,
The ordinals and cardinals and primes,
Chapter and verse, the tally marks and logs,
Denominators, numerators, lined
And rhyming in the diagrams and schemes
Derived from elemental paradigms,
Spellbound orthographies, broken ground maintained
Until the end of particle and star.

4

And just before you left us for a state
From which there is no waking, that last place
Of sleep and breath, you motioned for the chart
To be brought back once more. Then your good hand,
Guided by magic, science, or providence
Moved like a Ouija planchette, swivel-wheeled,
Fate's heart-shaped indicator prompted at will
Through grammar's fractions, lettered formulae.

And there, where axioms and syntax blend
Like lights above a clouded winter dawn,
You found your way along the road you came
From our first home and lasting habitude,
Those old geographies of soul and mind
Beyond the posted gates, your only toll
A solitary scansion of the land,
The layered tracings, ghostly palimpsests,
That chart and board a Ptolemaic map,
Four corners marked like heaven's windy zones,
A grinning sun, a moon close-lipped, serene,

Two matched pentangle circles, ringed by stars
In a galactic dance, the striking fires,
Bright ciphers of the Nothing and the All
Worded in night and silence, carried across,
Radiant declarations, pilots ablaze
Against a No Man's Land that no one knows,
Direct reflections, certainties unguessed,
One word just like a code-blue button — HELP —
HELLO that only others needed now,
And three for dying: GOODBYE, NO, and YES.

Clockwise

after verse about the hours of the day by Katherine Pyle in Howard Pyle's children's storybook The Wonder Clock *(1887)*

And now at last I lay me down to sleep,
An old man in the winter of his years,
So cold at twilight, taking to his bed,
Well-tended by what memory sees and hears.

Upon a hook within the family room
A wall clock marks the hours with its chimes
That comfort me, a widower alone,
Drawn late to other hours in other times.

My wife long gone to ashes, dust and bone,
Our children grown and scattered — I retired
To dwell inside some mellow pensiveness
That took deep hold as my past life expired.

And thus I lie in dark beneath a quilt
My Mary sewed from patches, odds and ends
That match a chronicle of days and ways
My clockwise mind recalls, then sifts and blends:

This stiffened shoulder where each crying child
Would sleep to Mary's baby song I'd sing,
A song she made so simple, sweet, and mild
It was itself the comfort it would bring;

The box of recipes — a wedding gift,
Handwritten cards in script of friend and kin
Long done with needing larder, stove, or board,
Ink fading toward the state their souls are in;

But most, a chest of letters, photographs
That Mary culled and stored before her death,
In scents of pomander and potpourri,
Keepsakes all laced with ribbons and her breath.

Such clockwise thoughts possess me as the hands
Move round a face, a smiling sleepy moon,
Its catalogue of hours my book of time,
More storied nearer midnight than at noon.

And so I know that right here all along
Our common life was not a common thing
But worthy to be praised, like Mary's song,
That only I and silence now can sing.

Test Pattern

It filled the screen from midnight until dawn
After the late show, anthem, station sign
In those brief early days of innocence
When television broadcast black and white.

The pattern was rectangular, abstract,
Made up of wheels and numbers, blocks and lines
To measure shape, proportion, light and dark,
Its soundtrack shrill — the sine wave's monotone.

But centered at the top as pure décor
A chief in profile stared beyond the set
In eagle-feathered headdress, beaded shirt
With cheekbones high and eyes and lips severe.

Penciled in '38 for RCA
The chief looks dignified, and much concerned,
A guardian spirit troubled by his charge,
Fair meadowlands so near where badlands are.

For by the time his image was replaced
With blank plain color bars the episodes
Of which he seemed the genius were no more
Or ran in syndications few would see:

Leave It to Beaver, The Andy Griffith Show
Where fathers talked with sons of right and wrong
Or *Gunsmoke* where Matt shot an outlaw down,
Then said to Chester, "he was just no good."

And now when desperate housewives push aside
June Cleaver, Harriet Nelson, and Aunt Bee
And even primetime viewing is PG
We long for Adam, Hoss, and Little Joe.

*

Today test patterns have no further use
For stations that stay on throughout the night
With infomercials, soft porn, cable news —
No national anthem, sign off, sleep and peace.

And what of the chief? His card was thrown away
In a dumpster when wrecking balls knocked down
The RCA's old factory — then was saved —
Retrieved by one of the demolition crew.

And for a while he stayed — a nightlight shade —
Glowing toward dawn when children safely woke
On cartoon Saturdays as did their folks
Who saw his pattern flicker on the screen.

Many of the nation's television stations used the image of the Indian-head card
to be their final image broadcast when they signed off their analog signals for the
final time between February 17 and June 12, 2009, as part of the United States
digital television transition. . . . It was sold as a night-light from 1997 to 2005.
— Wikipedia

Modern Times

1

Goodbye, Dear

How seldom now do you begin with *Dear*,
Both warm and formal (civil) but a mere
First name — "David:" — like a *Sir* or *Madam*
Summons to a wayward child of Adam,
No salutation as in Saint Paul's Letters,
Your curt tone saying one should know his betters
As if you bid a servant or a beast,
And you in all these emails not the least
Aware of such abruptness being rude —
Public, private address grown crass and crude —
And so, in closing, I reply (hit *Send*)
Goodbye: And let this conversation end.

Toll Free

Ire ad gehennam!

Reception bad on my cable TV
I punch the 800-number. Technically
Pleasant, an artificial female voice
Says "Hi. I'm here to help you. Make a choice:
English? *Español?*" "Latin." "Choose again."
"English." "OK. Now we can start." (I'm in.)
"Let's try to find the problem." "Well . . ." I pause
Wanting to be precise while cause on cause
Is quickly listed for my "Yes" reply
Or cordless button-pushing as I pry
To get more than a word in though the toll
In time and patience, rising, tries the soul
Till "No"s, then silence, prompt a change in tone:
"I need my supervisor. Hold the phone
Two minutes." Twenty pass. A curt "Hello"
To which my Latin tells him where to go
As "thanks for calling but we seem unable
To understand the problem with your cable"
And "this call has been monitored . . ." play through,
Reception clear as church bells, ringing true.

Cholesterol

after Robert Herrick (1591-1674), Anglican priest and poet, and author
of the poems "His fare-well to Sack" and "The Welcome to Sack"

1

Farewell

My annual checkup and its blood work done
And three weeks' fast to drive bad numbers down
I swing by Popeye's for the day's first treat —
A box of spicy thighs, red beans and rice —
Proud of myself as I am every time
Crash dieting to avoid yearlong regimes
To please my doctor who renews those pills
That keep my old heart beating quiet and strong.
But two days later comes the dreaded call,
My G.P. preaching on the "good" and "bad"
Cholesterol — a morality play
Of chemicals with Blood Sludge as the Vice.
So now I run on the treadmill, do dead lifts,
And live on tofu, lettuce, and O'Doul's
Slimming until suspenders must be bought
To hold pants up around new buns of steel
And washboard abs young girls stare at again.
But, Lord, I'm sixty. What's this good health for?
To wander through a nursing home at ninety,
Then curl up like a fetus on the floor?

Welcome

And what's the rush? I've got a year of pills
Renewed and I can plead heredity —
My father who ran marathons at fifty
With numbers past two-forty like my own
(My draft number not even half that high!)
Or his own mother who approached the same
Yet died of sheer old age at ninety-five.
And what are my doctor's readings, pray tell,
My dietician's in the checkout line
Stocking up on vodka, cheddar, Boston butt?
So taking one last look at the weird thrill
Of a three-score-year-old body teenage lean
With half a head of hair, a mind half daft,
And wrinkles where old bullied muscles bulge,
I bid farewell to numbers I can't rhyme,
Then go eat in New Orleans at K Paul's —
Welcoming buttered bread, shrimp gumbo, Chardonnay,
Watching abs of iron relax toward abs of flab,
Just grateful I've had sixty years, and sod
This liver and the metabolic gods.

Walking Through Thibodaux

When we came here some forty years ago
I'd jog the bayou road in rain and sun —
Often to jeers, and dodging glass below
When drivers hurled pop bottles just for fun.

But then young doctors set up in the town
And got potbellied patients on a track
Or walking trail to bring their weight back down
And ward off early stroke or heart attack.

So now we greet each other when we meet
At dusk or dawn our headbands dropping sweat
On soaked-through tee shirts, then to quickened feet
That speed us toward our goal of health, and yet . . .

What is the final end toward which we move,
Both sick and well, whether we will or no?
A fate whose nature none of us can prove
But into whose vast trackless realm we go?

May be. Yet still we walk along and gaze
Amazed by dazzling pageants of the skies,
This ordered chaos, star trails set ablaze
Toward which the aster blossoms while it dies.

And so, perhaps, we sojourn after all —
Though worlds like glass may shatter, doubters jeer —
Toward Love, the Great Physician, who will call
Our hearts to health beyond each sweated tear.

Town and Country

Aesop transposed to North and South Louisiana

A city mouse to country come
Picked at his cousin's store:
"How you can dine on rind and crumb,
Root, seed — and little more?

"Here in the north the fare is plain,
Its leavings make no treat,
Taken with rain from leak or drain,
Nothing like what I eat.

"Now visit me, and stay a while,
Down south in New Orleans,
The Quarter, where I live in style
And feast on high cuisines."

The country mouse replied in kind,
"I'm sorry your fine palate
No pleasure finds in bits of rind,
Hock, cracklin, or poke sallet.

"I've been content to have my share
From garden, garbage, table,
Mulch pile, bin, barn — whatever's there.
I live as I am able.

"Yet to return the courtesy
Of your brief visit here,
I'll come, somewhat reluctantly,
To share in your good cheer."

So both mice in a farm truck rolled
From field to river side,
And in a docked boat's cargo hold
They found a place to hide.

"These boxes packed with scuppernong
And peach will have to do
To nibble as we float along
Eluding rat and crew."

So said the town mouse who had tasted
Crawfish étouffée,
Shrimp sauce piquant, Turducken basted,
Bowls of crème brûlée.

"Well, I'm content with well enough,
The wheat seed or the tare,"
His cousin countered — grumpy, gruff,
"I just wish we were there."

And when they were the town mouse led
The way from boat to dock,
Then to his Quarter townhouse sped
Past gate and bar and lock.

And on a table still uncleared
Of silverware and plate
The remnants of a meal appeared.
The mice were not too late.

They tried, with appetites robust,
Broiled oysters on a tray,
Roast lamb with Creole mustard crust,
Then sipped absinthe frappé.

A sound. The cousins, as one mouse,
Pricked ears, and that was that,
Set on by guardians of the house,
Two mastiffs and a cat.

The city mouse took to his hole,
Cramped in a damp moss bed,
While north to a nest of straw and boll
His country cousin fled.

"I'd rather take my chances here,"
The city mouse declared,
"With dog and cat — and trout Meunière —
From rotten parings spared!"

But in the north his cousin fed
On pig ear, tongue, and jowl,
Happy with scraps and moldy bread,
Eye out for hawk and owl.

*

So, north and south, we live and die,
Enjoying, while we can,
Chicken and dumplings, mayhaw pie —
Andouille and boudin —

Though deep in pine flat, cypress slough,
We hear a raptor's call,
Who cooks for me? Who cooks for you?
Who cooks for you a-l-l?

4:00 A.M.

in memory of Philip Larkin (1922-1985)

That was the time you'd claim
And make your own
When dreaming fails and leaves
Us each alone,

No star-crossed lover lost
In sex and sweat
Or Hector braced for dawn
With archers set

Or Lear upon the heath
Raging but this:
An old man in the dark
Groping toward a piss.

The last line echoes Larkin's poem "Sad Steps," line 1.

October Oaks Revisited

of the water oaks at 607 Lafourche Drive, Thibodaux, Louisiana,
first written about in my poem "October Oaks"
— The Burning Fields, *1991*

Now twenty years have gone.
The oaks have gone as well,
Their sawdust on the lawn
Where trunk by trunk they fell

Long after my first verse
That praised them in their prime
Though even then the curse
Of star-dust claimed the rhyme

For in that mating-ground
Where crickets cried unseen
And shadows without sound
Moved through St. Augustine

The oaks would age and fail,
Pressed hard by flailing wind
In storms that left them frail,
Then given to their end.

The Book of Life

In stock a while, condition — fine,
No typo, blot, creased page, or line
Unjustified,
Its margins wide,
A classic, clean design:

This book of poems — set apart,
The printer's craft, the maker's art —
Was put one day
On layaway,
A dollar down to start.

At last the book became the boy's
Whose Lincoln Logs and Tinker Toys —
Then battle games,
Play's other claims —
Had given up their joys . . .

And at the end of Seven Ages —
Turning years and turning pages —
Working toward dust
As all boys must
He drew Old Adam's wages.

And what of poems so well borne
On pages spotted, browned, and torn —
Wisdom in time
In rhythm, rhyme —
By fingers smudged and worn?

Its crisp dust jacket long since lost,
Its spine's gilt title — foiled, embossed —
Flaking and stained,
Boards warped, joint-strained,
The book was sold at cost.

Yet verse sewn tight in signature
Unthreading now, will still endure —
Columned in print,
A spine unbent —
Taut lines its ligature.

Churches

North Louisiana, the late 1980s

Where nothing can be other than it was
— John Finlay, "The Wide Porch," 1984

a thing cannot be other than it is
— Aristotle, Posterior Analytics

1

In that first place from which the memory
Calls up in words the image of a thing
As what it was, is, ought, and has to be
I see affixed atop a concrete block
By marble graves and gravel parking lot
An old bell without belfry, yoke, or rope,
No longer rung though ghostly echoes toll
Forever for a church that isn't there.

The new church building has its own new bells,
Recorded sounds computer-timed to chime,
Thick red brick walls, low roof, bare windows squared,
Shut tight to trap the regulated air
Of central heat and cooling, no more need
For funeral home fans with winter scenes —
December's Driskill Hill in cresting snow —
Or iron potbellied stoves the deacons stoked
With logs of woodpile oak and hickory.

The worshippers there now seem satisfied,
Their Bibles in the language of the day,
Most sewn in cloth, as always, but a few
With cover angels smiling wing to wing
Or flowers loud in paperback pastels,
The simple hymns, Jehovah's jingling themes,

A happy hopping dot that shows the way
Through verses scrolled on giant projector screens,
The altar call's "Just As I Am," the same,
If lilting toward I Am from Need To Be,
The pews quite different, though, the contoured backs,
The cushioned seats, the smooth white solid pine.

It wasn't always so, for when that bell
Now on the ground rang swinging clean and clear
The pews were straight-backed, slatted, dark-stained, hard,
Their holders fit for glad and solemn psalms
In hymnals filled with Heaven, Hell, and Sin,
No Purgatory but a guilt unpurged
Till soul was born again alone and here
Where star-falls scar the dark with blemished light,
Even their grave elation circumscribed,
Inquisitors suspecting everything —
That self-denial was a kind of pride —
And in rough country hands, soft-leather bound,
Inerrant in its wanderings through tongues,
Pages opaque and silky, strong and thin,
A stately Jacobean Sacred Writ,
Black Bibles that a king had authorized,
Red words a greater king had bled to say.

And there, subsistence farmers, hunger-lean,
Raised up the first church house in those stark years
Between Petersburg's trenches and the Marne's —
The longleaf pine cut down for walls and floor,
Then planed and notched, doors locked with heavy keys,
The rooftree-rafters' sharp-pitched angled arch,
Tall windowpanes, blank gold, green, purple, blue,
A belfry's winding steps and maiden bell.

Inside, before the choir, the pulpit stood,
The holy focal point, and, at its foot,
No altar for high rites of flesh and blood,
Only a modest Table of the Lord,
A place for trays of tiny grape juice cups
And tidbit crackers scattered patternless,
No wine or bread made more with mystery,
And on the table's apron, in relief,
A plain command, the almost fasting feast
They kept: "This do in remembrance of me."

2

And there they felt a steady beckoning
Through seasons of creation and their lives
Drawing them ever onward, pew by pew,
Through north Louisiana when they heard
The tollings and the tellings of the bell.

The back pew first where now and then a child
Would cry to reach beyond the baptistery,
Its waters of the Jordan warm and calm,
The farther shore a mural, Adam's land,
Lambs grazing safe in spring's soft meadow grass,
And all along the cemetery fence
Unbruised magnolia blossoms opening slow
In April when the eastern phoebe leaves.

The older children, restless, further up
Doodling in the Bible coloring books,
Playing footsy under pews as prayers went on,
Girls teasing boys, the giggle-whispering,
Long sermons like eternity to them,
Light-bladed glades outside, their native place,
Looking past John the Baptist to a creek

In which they laughed and splashed through mayhaw days,
The summer herons green along the streams,
Striking quick minnows, stalking almost still.

Then teens and young adults seeing themselves
Slinging the stone that split Goliath's brow
Or dancing like a naked shepherd king
Or in The Song of Songs, their kisses spiced
With camphor, saffron, myrrh, and spikenard,
And in the Dove that seemed a turtledove
Cooing to woo and aching for its mate
Where Jesus rises drenched in sinlessness,
Rose pink so near, unfolding in its rose,
Jays making raucous flocks with mockingbirds,
Male sparrows courting females, feathers preened,
Driving off hawks from eggs in nesting time.

Next, in the middle pews, the middle-aged
Between dependent children, parents, pressed,
Too late to turn back now, so far to go,
Their first and second childhoods distant dreams,
The sun moving up to and through its noon,
Its firestorms flaring west of Galilee,
Kisatchie's asters tossed in autumn wind,
The scarlet ibis climbing toward the Gulf.

And last, in pews near table, pulpit, choir
The old who faintly hear the cries behind
Yet gaze in silent calm beyond the plains
Of Canaan to the Great Sea and their graves,
Torn spider webs hung frosted stone to stone,
Snow egrets over fields of virgin snow,
White berries on the poison mistletoe.

3

And by such pews and bells we come to know
Each season of the body and the soul,
The ways of winter moons and summer suns,
The progress of the far-cast gathered stars
Both wandering and constant by design,
Appearing thus for us, seen as we see,
Our granted vantage point this human pew,
Dear-bought and stained with more than human blood,
The universe a temple, stellar-belled,
Its music fire, its fire a light that sings:
And we who praise are ringers of the things
Just as they were, are, ought, and have to be,
Calling the congregations near and far
To common rites of life, death, peace, and war,
The parts of bells a part of what we are —
The crown, head, shoulder, waist, mouth, lip, and tongue —
Sounding out all our days and nights profound
As does a bell well grounded, stilled for years
Yet tolling in remembrance where we dwell
Forever in a church that's always here.

Calling Down the Birds

in memory of Louisiana naturalist Caroline Dormon (1888-1971)

You saw them just the way they really were,
Those flowers in your gardens and the wild,
Studied, preserved, in earth and paint and words,
The naturalist and artist of one mind.

The red woodbine and orange-yellow phlox,
Greenbrier, blue larkspur, nodding indigo,
The violet oxalis — rainbow names —
A covenant in pastoral catalogue.

You knew the birds as well, the goldfinch, wren,
The swallow, warbler, sparrow and the food
They loved to eat, calling them from the trees
To peck up at your feet the sprinkled seed.

And you would stay at Briarwood — birthplace, home —
Secluded in a wold's uplifted hills,
Your cabin, grounds, a modest green estate
By wisdom and solicitude maintained.

And there some April dawns a pineland quiet
Would draw you on toward spots in partial shade
Good for Celestials, common once, now rare
In north Louisiana's well-drained clays.

Their sky-blue petals graceful on the stem,
They open in midmorning, shrivel at noon,
Then die before their first and only day
Darkens toward far-off clusters of the stars.

And you remembered how their meadowlands
Once flowered around Old Shreveport to its edge,
Now ringed with plants and neighborhood escapes
Lying like slabs above the dusty bulbs.

*

I came from Shreveport often as a boy
To visit kin close by you, in Saline,
And I would ask to share your solitude
By following and watching for a day.

You taught me birds you named by sight and song
And let me smell new cuttings taking root,
Species at threat that you would propagate,
Their wildness spared and thriving in your care.

And once, when I brought down those early poems
You read and complimented, being kind,
Sensing how I was trying to say my way
Back home to that same place you never left,

You had me stand apart, yet almost near,
Then called the autumn birds from bough and sky
To come to earth and eat Celestial seeds,
This time from open hands you lifted up

Toward feathers cloudy-black and iris-bright,
A kingdom needing peace, a saving grace,
A mixed flock growing larger by your love,
Still trusting that first promise you had made.

Porches

*Village of Saline, Bienville Parish, North Louisiana
at my late maternal grandparents' house*

The sand and gravel road, smooth asphalt now,
Passes beside the church and sunken stones
Of kin both dead and living yet awhile
In memories of one who left and stayed.

I slow down for those fields recalled and seen —
The cultivated, fallow, undisturbed —
Shift my old standard into neutral gear,
Then quietly glide toward stillness and the drive.

Others have owned this house for sixty years,
And though my home is here in every sense,
Possessing and possessed I cannot step
At will upon a transferred property.

So rolling down the window I look out
Binding in mind what's gone with what remains,
Then walk up to a gatepost where I wait
For shades to gather thin in autumn air.

And there, in seasons blending without end —
The bloom and fruit, oxalis and pecan —
On that deep porch between the hall and yard
I see myself and listen, man and child,

To voices long conversant with a world
Made up of things that have their place and ways
In calendar and catalogue and rhyme,
The holy days of ordinary time:

Spring's golden corydalis, white-topped sedge,
The yellow evening primrose, yellow worts —
St. Peter's and St. John's — in summer dusk,
Wisteria in thickets by the streams,

The sprawling moss verbena — purple, rose —
By early August done, October's frost-
And chain-leaf asters, winter possum haw,
And dandelion puffballs at winter's end.

And where these thrive and die without a sound
Pine warblers nest unseen in tallest pines,
Their high-pitched trill forever coming down
While from the last few open longleaf groves

Now passing with the passing hillside farms
Lark-sparrows sing in elegy and leave
Stump fields of their unsettled breeding-place,
Searching in other woods for native ground.

Such things I take to heart and keep in mind,
Beholding and beholden, in their gift,
Each one a porch — a station and a way,
The inward and the outward reconciled,

The fathomed patterns matching, world and word,
Like mockingbirds whose mimicking in spring
Sweetens into a single autumn song,
By Choctaws called "the bird of many tongues."

And so I leave the gatepost and the drive
In treetop light from afternoon's low sun
That blinds me in the rear-view mirror's glass,
The future now reflected in the past

Along this sand hill road where crest to crest
Pines rise sky-high in colonnades of fire.

Fairgrounds

Louisiana State Fair, Shreveport, October 1961

after Philip Larkin's "Show Saturday"

Late morning and the first cars roll up,
Motioned into their parking spots by staff
Who point down a roped way toward ticket booths
Either side of the clicking turnstile bars.

The children go through first, racing ahead
Into a place where fantasies come true;
The parents listen for the rising pitch
Of barkers holding toys out from their stalls.

But it's too soon for that and carnies still
Stay busy picking up last night's debris:
Matted cotton candy, deflated balloons,
Popcorn scattered like seed, crushed Dixie cups.

And so, to start, the Ag-Show, on its own,
A harvest festival of crops and stock,
Now set apart from midway games and rides
Long since the main attractions of the fair.

The parish champions are on display,
A town of temporary tent-barns, pens,
Black Hereford and Angus — bull and cow —
State winners with blue ribbons garlanded.

Some city boys and girls in shorts and T's
Printed with Mickey Mouse or Donald Duck
Marvel at beasts both magical and real
Serenely chewing cud above the dung.

Off by themselves, under a bigger tent,
New tractors gleam, posed like showroom cars.
Pamphlets are given out by salesmen dressed
In Caterpillar yellow, John Deere green.

They nod toward a corner where an angled fence
Rails off a nineteenth-century wooden plow,
Its iron blade dulled and rusted, handles, smooth,
Worn down to fit a single pair of hands.

The children, hungry, tug at their parents' arms.
They're restless, and it's getting well past noon.
Concession stands entice them with the smells
Of corndogs, burgers, onion rings, and fries.

And now they're ready for the carousel,
Holding tight to the ponies on their posts
Going up and down and round and round
And that's enough: it's time to go back home.

Soon afternoon and twilight bring the teens,
Older ones driving, younger ones dropped off
By fathers, who'll return for them at ten.
The carnival and night grow bright and loud.

And everywhere thrill after thrill draws crowds,
The Teacups spinning and the Tilt-A-Whirl,
Bumper Cars, the Wipeout, and the Whip,
The Wild Mouse with its unbanked hairpin curves,

Playing with gravity, jolting space and time,
The riders still dazed as they find their way
Down platform stairs onto the firm flat ground,
Some whooing, giddy, others, throwing up.

The line is slow outside the House of Mirrors,
(An even flow so panic doesn't start),
A maze of see-through panes, reflecting glass,
And doorless frames that seem to lead nowhere

Then suddenly confront one with a form
Known, yet unfamiliar, bending out or in,
Frightening and laughable — the mixing tears —
Torso collapsed, a bulging wide-stretched mouth.

The carousel outgrown, not wanting to leave
Just yet the revelers head for the Ferris wheel,
Couples among them snuggling in the seats
Spoke rods lift north, each stopping at the top.

And when the gentle back-and-forth is stilled,
They look down at the midway, up toward stars,
The wheeling lights and music, in their spheres,
The fairs of earth and heaven almost one.

But then a slow descent to the exit ramp,
The long way round to reach the parking lot,
To make it last, the couples hand in hand.
And as they pass the Ag-Show tents and pens

They see the cows asleep on hay and sand,
At home and whole where others once had been,
The winners with blue ribbons garlanded,
A childhood memory come back again.

Let all this be forever as it is.

Biographer: A Life

in memory of Mark Royden Winchell (1948-2008),
author of biographies of Donald Davidson and Cleanth Brooks

Leaning through silence to a dead man's mind
— Dick Davis

He sits amid the facts he's gathered in
From interviews, books, archives, scattered prose
Mastered at last so recollection's pen
Can resurrect the dead by what he knows.

He minds the many pitfalls of his art,
Wary of how some storytellers err
In idolizing, tearing men apart,
Iconoclast or hagiographer.

He must engage, yet shuns the quick surmise,
With passion for those cool exactitudes
He isolates from hearsay, myths, and lies,
Tactful and tentative as he intrudes.

And when the work of long hard years is done
As chapters of his life in holograph,
He'll rest with each dead man whose race he's run,
Their hours enshrined in timeless epitaph.

Lee in Darkness

Lee, "a public nuisance"

Not marble nor the gilded monuments . . .
      — Shakespeare, Sonnet 55

It is history that teaches us to hope.
      — Robert E. Lee

A century and more he stood alone
Atop his column, elevated, grave,
Arms folded, in full military dress,
Looking hard north from where "those people" came.

Now workers come, in bulletproof vests and masks,
Lifted up toward his feet by a yellow crane,
Lashing him with blue straps, straining to turn
Tight bolts that held him steady in his place.

And soon the crew would hoist, then bring him down
Where civil war had broken out again —
Our own Fire-Eaters, Abolitionists
Shouting half-truths, flags clashing at the base.

Such wars displace old statues, raise up new,
Which will themselves be toppled, shattered, ground
Into the very dust to which the dead
Like columns that exalt them must return.

Lee was no "marble man," no man of bronze,
And would have been dismayed to find himself
Set on so high a pillar, so revered
By some as almost saint or demigod.

And yet how few have characters less flawed:
This man whom Lincoln offered the command
Of a whole army to subdue the South
(His statue raised for that inside the Dome!)

This sinner who not far from a black man knelt
There at the rail while other whites held back
Until by his example shamed and led
To join him at the Table of the Lord.

The public is not ready for the truth,
So cautioned Lee when southern flags were furled,
This man who did his duty, kept his faith
That time might soften fury into love:

Old soldiers reenacting Pickett's Charge —
The Jubilee of Gettysburg that fell
The year before the Great War — graybeards all,
Rebs crossing blood-sown ground toward Yankee tears and hugs.

But, Lee, "a public nuisance," is removed
By politicians, men in vests and masks,
From civic space to city warehouse hauled,
Consigned for now to darkness not his own.

Yet on that pillar where so long he stood
There still remains the measure of the man,
A presence some can sense and none disturb
Sculpted in tempered memories and words.

The War Between the Dreams

Old slave and planter graves a flight apart
For thrushes eating seeds of grass and yew,
The unmarked plots and plots with dates and names
Too weatherworn to trace and know in stone,
Bones sinking toward a spring no well can reach,
600,000 dead for whom the War
Has long since ended and will never end,
The blue and gray at peace beneath the green,
The Deep South vultures riding updrafts north,
Smelling the human meat two states away —
Cold Harbor in the rank and columned air —
Flocking to open feasts of bowel and blood,
Blacks joining their red cousins, circling high,
Then swooping and alighting, plucking eyes
From bloated bodies hissing in their gore,
Confederate and Federal the same,
Cain slaying Abel, Abel slaying Cain,
The first fruits and the last of staff and scythe,
Of muskets and repeaters, bayonets,
The wounded paralyzed between the lines,
Crows tugging at their guts as they looked down,
The cries for "Mother!" heard and yet unheard,
Prophetic epitaphs in diaries
Of the dead: "June 3. Cold Harbor. I was killed."
Pride and compassion clashing through a truce,
The colors of both armies on the ground,
The Stars and Stripes beside the Southern Cross,
The standard-bearers leading, first picked off,
And somewhere in a clearing hidden still
From this new restless unaccustomed mind
That cannot now remember or forget,

Among a people neither lost nor found,
Each year the older birds, the winter scouts,
Come back to claim familiar nesting sites
Beside the sisters — beans and squash and corn —
The planted standards neither flown nor furled
But steadfast in the time of egg and seed,
Gourd poles, for the purple martins, hung with gourds.

The Turning of the Cannon

They gleam there wheel to wheel on that last ridge,
Keeping us from the valleys of our birth
From which we have been driven, field by field,
Leaving dead kin to hold our native earth.
And yet like shades dissolving dark in dawn
Those people seem as abstract as their maps
That simplify our tale to their idea —
This barn we built, that chapel where we wed,
Each family plot railed off by spike and yew —
Just dots or patches hatched, not real and true.

Now fault lines cross and part on common ground —
Matter made absolute in chattel slaves
Chained to the land or urban sleights of hand
That pay in scrip of rhetoric and debt —
But in the heat of battle such cold facts
Are lost in fumes, confusion, civil war
Though not on us, hunkered in great live oaks
Whose limbs in wind conduct night's silent fires,
Old monotones of star-scored earth and sky,
Grand anthems of the essence and the bone.

And though these stately measures fade away
When shot tears hot through smoke that will not clear,
And we are cast as cast-out demons in
Simplistic allegories of our foe,
We'll charge once more their shifting lines and guns
With bayonet and clan-yell fixed, then raised,
Our muzzleloaders taking down whole crews
That man those massed Napoleons we'll turn
To drive them one fine April from the ridge
That slopes toward the Old Republic's Washington.

The Voyage of Pytheas

in memory of Allen Tate (1899-1979)

We thought we saw some distant citadel
On those sheer cliffs of Thule where we sailed,
First mapping craggy coasts of Cornwall, Wales,
Then north into uncharted deeper seas.

Ice-crusted bluffs broke up from breaking spray,
Their bottom rocks thrust downward toward the core,
And on bleak heights white birds we could not name
Left eggs in crevices where blizzards roar.

And we, who, from the south, knew how its noon
Soaked orchards ripe with olives, grapes, and figs,
Now stared on barest stone that blocked the stars
Whose light dripped salt from glazing oars and rigs.

And when slow polar swells raised up our ship
Between night's sunward sea and seaward sun
We glimpsed the final limit of the world
As fire fell curled and frozen from those walls

Where we had flung it. Then, terrified, we turned
Our prow around, bore toward the middle sea,
By Thule's winds brought home to Thule here —
Late hoarfrost on the tender lemon trees!

In the Beggar's Palace

after passages in Books XXI and XXII of The Odyssey

Like a singer long familiar with his lyre
Who loops the twisted sheep gut, bound at tail and bar,
Turning a new peg until it tunes the cord,
He strung the great bow, bending its limbs with ease,
The test-pluck sounding high like flights of swallow song,
The shaft zinging clean through twelve ax-handle eyes.

A beggar no more, aiming true with measured rage,
He targeted at will each uninvited guest
Who swilled his wine, gulped food, bedded his ready maids
All night, while his pressed queen drew the slowly woven strands,
Saved by a web's deceit, but then betrayed, undone
Till bronze-tipped arrows threading the air sped home.

Soon those who had given themselves to would-be kings
Unwillingly scrubbed blood from upset tables, chairs
And dragged slain lovers off, their corpses trailing gore,
Then after were hemmed in hard by yard and wall,
Like thicket-birds come to roost, trapped in a net,
Thrushes and doves flushed toward another kind of sleep.

And there, pulling plied cable, taut from post to dome,
Set high enough so a barely lifted foot
Could just brush its shadow moving on the ground,
Telemachus had them bow to a noose's loop
That tightened until they writhed (though not for long),
Snapped neck-bones, muscles convulsed . . . in stillness limp.

Then Odysseus' old nurse, who knew him by the scar,
Brought purifying sulfur, torches dipped in tar,
Blue flames from the yellow crystals melting red

In trays along the fumigated hall, the dead
Suitors finished, a body of work made so
By a crafty king who strung a poet's bow.

Testament of the Elder Son

Now his elder son was in the field . . .
— *Luke* 15: 25

for the Southern Agrarians

The twilight spreads through barley, wheat, and rye
Bending in winds that never stay the same
While I, a posted ghost who raised them high
Still hear the swaying grasses say my name.

I bear the ancient burden of the earth
As steward of the corn and egg and seed
And understand what bulging barns are worth
When famine sows the land with fearful need.

And here I stood some forty years ago
Still pulling out the tares from bearded wheat
At nightfall when there rose up from below
Wild music for the prance of dancing feet.

Then leaving these high terraces I found
My father's house aroused by wine and song,
My grain-fed calf spit-roasted, turning round,
My younger brother robed among the throng.

I shunned that unjust feast but sent in word
Which drew my father out while I complained,
Though he, in his warm mercy, barely heard,
So flush with lush forgiveness unrestrained.

He said again that all he had was mine —
As if it could be otherwise by law —
Although a third was gone among the swine
Whose latest feeder's new gold ring I saw.

Strong drink, the dice, the whores, the foreign gods,
Then famine in the land — he told his tale
That ended in a wallow's carob-pods
And in a revelry more fit for Baal.

Years passed, my father died, and I became
Sole owner of estates where I was born
Whose harvests long had granted me the same
Great stores of wine and cattle-flesh and corn.

A man of substance taking stock I paid
My wealthy sonless neighbor's bridal-fee
To have as mother of my sons a maid
Erotic in her comely modesty.

Together we grew middle-aged, then old,
With sons enough to work a fertile land
Now doubled as my prudence had foretold
And daughters married well as I had planned.

And what of him for whom the calf was slain,
A rioter welcomed home with riotous dance?
He soon sought that far country once again,
His contrite heart no more than circumstance.

And when at last word came that he had died
Of drunkenness, disease, and poverty
I placed him with his father, side by side
In shallow graves beneath a carob tree.

The Hay Wain

after the painting by John Constable (1776-1837)
1821
oil on canvas

Midsummer noon: a tributary stream
Glides slowly by warm meadows toward the Stour,
And there, fording the shallows set agleam

By cloud-light rippling in the shaded hour
A hay wain stops to cool its wheels' iron bands
Before a place the bank-side trees embower.

The wain will round this spong toward pasturelands
Where distant figures, bending, rake the hay
Later to stack and bale with practiced hands

While deep in reeds, his pole and line in play,
An angler stands as mated ducks glide near,
All waiting for the fish that swim their way.

Almost unchanged, Lott's Cottage is still here
Just as it was three hundred years ago,
And from its porch, extending like a pier,

A woman stoops where currents coldly flow,
Filling her jug as chimney smoke drifts white
Far from a pot hearth-logs smolder below.

The watered team will move on, bearing right,
But now the driver rests against the wain's
Slats added to low boards for space and height;

Meanwhile, a younger helper, rising, strains
His voice and arm to hail a dog that turns
Toward him alone under the coming rains.

Above, a brown cloud none as yet discerns
Moves down over the windrows winds explore,
Leaving wet stalks to dry when noonday burns.

Unseen — because the painter stood before —
His father's mill, grinding the wheat to flour,
The family business John chose to ignore

Though want forced him to render, tense and dour,
Those country-gentry portraits he could sell
When few would buy his landscapes of the Stour,

A realm at peace in which his mind might dwell,
No church or castle anywhere in sight,
Only a pastoral world he loved so well

That here at last he got it wholly right,
No restless, fretted strokes but things serene,
Unmannered in the equalizing light.

Bringing Home Cows After Eden

North Louisiana

Through cover crops of winter oats and rye
Along a trail first cut by buffalo
A farmer leads his milk cows from the fields
After a day let loose in stubble hay.

The cattle egrets stay to dig up grubs
Under a shallow frost-line cows disturb
Grazing by sun and moon and by the light
From stars that died a billion years ago.

The starlight brightens deep in eventide
As creatures move along the ancient way
Until the man discerns familiar shapes
Of gate, trough, well, coop, wallow, pen, and barn.

The cows bed down and sleep in bovine peace,
Not yet gone dry and tagged for the slaughter-chute
While on a hayloft rafter, perched alert,
A barn owl waits for rustling in the hay.

Shepherdess with Her Flock and Dog

after the painting by Jean-François Millet (1814-1875)
1863-1865
black conté crayon and pastel with pen and black ink on beige laid paper

"Make more idylls," his Paris dealer said,
Poor Alfred Sensier, caught in between
The artist and a public he had shocked:
That grim *Man with a Hoe* the year before . . .

And thus you read the classics once again,
Your Île de France absorbing as its own
Theocritus' green Sicily and Cos
And Virgil's island-hearted Arcady:

These sheep at peace, still huddled as they graze,
A dog alert yet easy in its stance,
A shepherdess, so comely and serene,
Head bent to tell her threadings as she works

Her needles though her staff is now at rest
As if she dreamed of Saturn's Golden Age,
Nor is she far from Eve who calmly led
The first sheep out of Eden when she fell —

This human muse — both simple and profound,
Where longing and belonging dwell as one
With forest, plain, and field, near Barbizon,
What Vincent saw and called your "holy ground."

To Her Who Bears These Verses

Goddess, fertile and waiting,
Maker of our creating,
Coming to me in slumber
Deeper than name and number:
I waken to our mating.

My need become your need,
You draw my words like seed
Till blooming white with aster
Against the stars' disaster
Your womb bears out my creed

That *word-thing* is the kenning
Uncoupled by a sinning
When like from like first wandered
And poets only pondered
The hyphen's quiet unpinning.

Yet when in wakeful dreaming
So seamlessly beseeming
You answer me unbidden
Revealing what is hidden
I feel a love redeeming

Each cloven metaphor
Where breakers mark the shore
Of time and space upwelling
In rhymes made more compelling,
More telling than before.

Infinitives

do it for ancient love
> — Gloucester to the Old Man in *King Lear*

most modern English usage guides have dropped the objections
to the split infinitive
> — Wikipedia

in memory of H.J. Sachs (1904-1983)

You never tired of telling us again
That story, when, in 1932,
Hearing the atom had been split at last,
You slowly walked the English building halls
Dreading a bomb's apocalypse to come,
Then glimpsed as you passed an open classroom door
A colleague lecturing freshmen on the split
Infinitive, still going by the book,
An old-guard battle-ax grammarian
On separating particle and verb.

Years later, in the '60s' Sturm und Drang
We read through *Lear* with you as wandering guide,
Chain smoking Kents, injecting politics,
And we, like Kent, attentive to a king,
Some of us on the front row with a light
And cigarettes to offer should you draw
The last ash to its filter and be out,
Rapt by the situation's irony,
A split infinitive, the atom split,
That colleague whose priorities you mocked.

For, after Hiroshima, you would ask,
Why care about a verb kept from its sign
Or study Keats' "To Autumn" while the fields

Hide silos ripe with warhead mega-bombs,
Each one a key click from a blast beyond
Fat Man's and Little Boy's a thousand times,
A fatal knowledge we cannot unknow,
Forever undisarmed, these latter days
Always October 1962,
Kennedy grim on black and white TV.

And you would pace like Lear upon the heath
In storms of atoms and the atmosphere —
Particles, stars, all forced from centering rings —
Then hold up hanged Cordelia to arraign
High "Justicers" enthroned above their laws,
Impassive while the showerheads spread gas
Not far from ovens fed with human flesh
Till evening when the camp guards cleaned their pipes
Under a lamp's soft glow, neat whiskey near,
And Mozart on the crackling radio.

Yet history still may be a tale well told,
A wedding, not a funeral, at its end,
The timeless twining in and out of time
Sewing the book of hours of things and tongues
Where *was* and *is* and *will be* make one tense
Beyond all tenses, every part of speech
Incisive and precise, if bravely placed,
The ethicist and rhetor standing firm
In testament before a firing squad
They bless with prayers and crossings by the wall.

But then, on 9/11, when the planes
Flew into towers that fell into themselves,
Firebirds consumed with shearing wings aflame
And only ashes rising from their ash,
The word came down to let our classes go

If the stunned students felt they could not bear
To try to learn with terror in their heads —
Jumpers to streets a hundred floors below —
And yet I walked the halls past empty rooms
To hold my class in writing poetry.

And as I went along I thought of you
Who many years before had overheard
That exacting grammarian and judged
A solecism something trivial . . .
So when I reached the desktop podium,
Opening the worn handbook to a page
Turned down at our last meeting, I looked up,
Then told those who had come that they could leave
For family, priest, friend, counselor, smoke or drink
Though I would teach if even one remained.

I quoted Auden on the death of Yeats,
The poet's role to pity, heal, and praise,
Mastering the craft and going by the book,
And though they all were shaken, lost for words,
No one rose to go as I stressed again
That rules of verse can set a poet free —
Caesura, line break, meter, rhyme, and stave —
Significance bound up in space and time
Like particled infinitives unsplit
In atom, grammar, host, the maker's art.

And while I spoke I felt you standing there,
Your love for "unaccommodated man"
An "ancient love" like blinded Gloucester saw,
Still fixed in syntax and its hierarchies,
Those old subordinations, phrase and clause,
Philology, the chain of being, wed,
Though we would ask, "Is this the promised end?"

"Or image of that horror?" "Fall and cease!"
If words should fail and language come to harm
When dying kings hold daughters in their arms.

Ordinations

priest, poet

Receive this Bible as a sign . . .
— The Book of Common Prayer (1979), 534

Younger than I by nearly forty years,
He stands for examination, then kneels,
The bishop laying hands upon the head
Of one who prays for strength to rise again,
Holding on tight to a Bible, the gift
A bishop gives to all whom God has called
To preach the Word and offer bread and wine.

Here in the pews, near three score years and ten,
I see myself — and not — in that young man,
For I was also called, ordained, my gift
Not given by a bishop but a voice
That left me with the silence of the page
And language from a common lexicon,
The Holy Spirit blessing *grape* and *grain*.

An Exmoor Tale

Toward dawn he made his way by bay and cliff
Into the Brendon Hills, journeying west
On through the Quantocks to collect a debt
From one who had ignored his many bills.

In town he had a shop with staple goods
And out of town a farm whose meats and greens
He sold with flour sifted from his grains
All native to a world he loved and knew.

And so he rode across the summer moors
With heather, ling, and whortleberry decked,
Glimpsing the elusive roe deer and the red
At daybreak in the distant hillside mist.

He knew the birds as well, by habit, name,
The scrub's grasshopper warbler, bred in heath,
Redpolls that nest on moorland edges deep
In sessile oaks, and, by the channel bays,
Snow buntings, ospreys, egrets, harriers
All fishing while long swells salted the caves.

And pushing on till dusk mile after mile
For hours intent on justice, recompense,
Fair dealing, and the holding to one's word
He reached at last an isolated farm,
Ill-tended, where his debtor could be heard
Behind that door on which the traveler knocked.

Slowly the door was opened and he gazed
Upon a face angelic yet distressed,

With eyes like wells of light but in a haze,
Skin pale against the dark brown feathery hair.

The man who came would enter a strange room
The other kept in twilight — candles, faint,
Illumining a pen, chair, table, page,
An empty glass still smelling of strong drink
And something else, some flavoring spice, or drug.

The two men spoke alone an hour or more,
Yet still the bills remained, though credit stopped,
And he who traveled far to balance books
Gave up on one he could not understand . . .

Then tiring far from town as night wore on
He headed for his farmstead closer by,
And there, as he had left them — hives and pens,
The bees and cows, and, in the heeded fields,
Green wheat just turning golden toward the fall.

The next day he wrote off the unpaid sum
And lived on toiling as he always had
In intimate blood kinship with the land.

Years later, someone showed him that small book
In which the debtor blamed him for a poem
Whose birth he'd interrupted with his knock.

And there he read of things he could not know
Except by correlation to a world
He nurtured as its substance nurtured him:
A holy river like the river Exe
Rising at Exe Head, flowing south through shale,
Unmeasured caverns Bristol Bays' deep caves
Below Great Hangman Cliff, an eastern mount

Dunkery Beacon, mystic honey-milk
Those hives and cows he tended long before
He'd be The Man from Porlock evermore.

Peasant Leaning on a Pitchfork

after the drawing by Jean-François Millet (1814-1875)
ca. 1848-1850 (Paris and Barbizon)
black conté crayon on paper
private collection, Europe

Midmorning, and the autumn harvest done,
Stubble burned, a young man rests a moment,
Leaning against his pitchfork as he dreams,
His head turned well away from waiting fields.

A slight smile, half-closed eyes tell of longing
For Paris and his story's happy end —
An artist painting pleasing country scenes —
O surely there in all those years to come!

But dumped beside him now, a pile of dung
The cowherds bring, his work to work it in
Until the soil stinks, ready for new seed,
This ground where men by human need are bound.

Not far, two older peasants, long resigned,
Toil on, their heads bent down toward spread manure,
Thinking of noon's brief sleep while line by line
Trees reach to brush the light in light brown sky.

The young man would not dream of being them
And cannot know as yet that there will be
No turning from this turning of the dung,
Bucolic in his urban fantasies.

Noonday Rest

after the picture by Jean-François Millet (1814-1875)
1866
pastel and black conté crayon on buff wove paper

High August noon and skies are cloudy-bright
Over young lovers sleeping in the shade
Of a huge rick their daylong labor made
Between the twilight hours of moon and sun.

The woman's cheek rests on her folded arms,
Smooth skin the wrinkling heat leaves cracked and dry.
The man's brow sweat is cooled by a tilted hat.
Their faces turn like wheat a tawny bronze.

Far off, cattle browse at a cart's tall wheels
Worn by the many rounds from plain to barn.
Nearby — one blade upon the other laid —
Two sickles, from the Iron Age come down.

The reapers gather grain-heads in a fist,
Then cut back toward themselves, the curving edge
Of tool and weapon wielded in the fields,
This battle of the harvest marked by Cain.

Their provenance — Millet's own history,
Early and late, the shady grove and glade,
The nymph and hero naked in the bays,
Embedded here almost too deep to see.

Peasant Woman Watering Her Cow

after the picture by Jean-François Millet (1814-1875)
ca. 1863
oil paint and black conté crayon on pink prepared canvas
dessin peint

Fall skies glow pink and golden on a ground
Prepared and worked — the canvas and the land —
Black bones of crayon drafts left showing through
These watercolor washes drawn in oils.

Late afternoon still lingers as it fades,
The sun's north rim descending to eclipse,
And all that moves or stays on Chailly Plain
Is blended in one dimming silhouette.

Along horizon lines of mind and earth,
Crossing a rise just on perception's edge,
A shepherd leads his straggling hollow flock
From scanty pastures home to feed on sleep.

And where the shades stain scrub a deeper green
Dead stunted trunks angle toward light and rain.
A woman walks on stones beside a pond,
Watching her cow drink water from the stars.

Lapped ripples crest and spread near skin-tight ribs,
Gaunt haunches, udders giving little milk.
A head's reflection noses toward the air.
From a full barn's loft-window no bale falls.

The moon protracts a single lighted claw.

The Stubble Burner

after the painting by Jean-François Millet (1814-1875)
ca. 1860
oil on canvas

Tired reapers gone to thresh and winnow seed,
A stubble burner comes, her task to light
Stalk-stumps cut down, then raked up into piles,
The fall's last harvest, given to the fire.

Some heaps are smoldering, smoke rising white
Toward buff-white clouds wheat golden in the sun.
The burner watches hard, her pitchfork tines
Ready to toss more straw on ash and spark.

She stokes black centers growing wide and low,
Bringing to flames the air they eat and breathe,
This Chailly peasant — but her profile Greek —
Her straight lips set beyond a frown or smile.

Her world is as she finds it, undisturbed
By dream or longing, fretting or regret,
And yet she seems Athene, looking on
As plumes spread west from Troy to Barbizon.

The turning year, her years, stay what they are
As season blends with season, flesh and earth,
The Sower and the Reaper soon to come,
The night a stubble field of scattered stars.

The Threshing Floor

in honor and in memory of Jean-François Millet (1814-1875)

Late autumn and the reaping, binding done,
Spent carters bring more sheaves to a threshing floor
Where flailers wait, long hours of work before,
As days grow short under the year's low sun.

The floor is stone — smoothed on the bedrock's head.
The flail is helve and swipple, clasp, and ring.
Each beater walks on stalks, his downward swing
Cracking the chaff whose grain is ground for bread.

Some seed, the best, is sown among the crows,
Cast out upon the fatal earth again
Where it will sink — till raised by warming rain —
Under the stubble-ash and winter snows.

                          *

And so the year for years went on and on
From season unto season toward the day
Machines were made to shake the seed away
From chaff no longer split by flail and stone.

Now thrashing cracks the atom to its core,
The mind a weapon flailing its own self,
While deep below the continental shelf
The Thresher stays unraised forevermore.

Yet here and there a weathered floor remains
Tilted, exposed to take the rain and wind,
Where, dead and ready, given to their end,
Winnowers toss aloft the ancient grains.

First Steps

*after preliminary sketches, the finished drawing, and the "pasteled" drawing
by Jean-François Millet (1814-1875)
1858-1866*

with quotations translated from letters written by Millet to his art dealer in Paris

Washed linens draped along a picket fence
Running beside the garden, house, and yard
Dry white against the greens of shrub and tree
Whose shades are conté gray on thread and board.

The garden has its own fence — like a toy —
A line of tiny sticks that barely stand,
A marker, not a barrier, a sign
For any who step over or around.

The autumn plants have wintered into spring —
Sprouts rising toward a light on melting snow —
Maturing, then dug up, a poor man's food,
Potatoes, carrots, turnips, cabbage, beets.

Nearby, a mother, bending from behind,
Steadies a little daughter set to walk,
While almost too far off for her to reach
The father kneels, his rough soiled hands stretched out.

And there, upon the edge of letting go,
The toddler takes a first step on her own,
Uncertain . . . fall after fall to come,
Making her way toward strong uplifting arms.

*

How long Millet would take to get this right,
Sketch after sketch to shape and place, and then,
The finished drawing, monochrome, composed
In "calm" he sought "to stop the rush of time."

And so the scene would "concentrate itself"
On "real essentials" — "catch the intimate" —
In these our common lives . . . a trusting child
Who like us all must learn to walk alone.

But in the 1850s few would buy
Such drawings — peasant life too stark and hard
To hang on paneled walls, near port, cigars,
In Paris, Boston, London, or New York.

And so, to stave off poverty and please
His dealer, Sensier, Millet "enhanced"
A picture he thought done in neutral tones,
Coloring in the lines with soft pastels.

Yet *First Steps* as he sold it, heightened, bright,
Depends on the perspective coming down
Draft after draft — black chalk across white sheets —
The father, mother, daughter, unenhanced,

Drawn closer to each other and their ground.

Reading Lesson

after the drawing by Jean-François Millet (1814-1875)
ca. 1860
black conté crayon on wove paper

St. Anne Teaching the Virgin
(1839, oil on canvas, current location unknown)

Cold light brightens the panes it passes through
Into a room where mother, daughter, sit,
The teacher in a chair, child on a bench,
Dawn sun illuminating face and page.

Around the figures warmly dressed in wool
Are crayon shades — sleep, waking, work, and play:
A made bed, sheet turned back, a pillow fluffed,
A feather duster hooked high on a wall,

A shelf with jars and bowls yet higher still,
A basket near the mother, raveled clothes,
And on the window ledge a propped-up doll
Blanketed, kissed, and left at lesson time.

The mother tilts a primer in her lap,
Inclining toward her child who leans to see
Each letter by a pointer singled out,
The ABCs of words and verses learned.

Millet, too, learned, in 1839,
His first submission — turned down by the Salon,
A painting in a drawing lost and found,
Bound pages in an artist's Book of Hours,

Color intoned, well grounded, hymning limned,
A story weaving in and out of time,

Psalters of Nazareth and Normandy,
St. Anne teaching the Virgin how to read.

Of Root and Bloom

for my daughter, Anna

As I recall, your second word was *flower*
That autumn when the purple pansies blew,
Time waking every season in its hour
Till reason's seed found fertile ground in you.

For eighteen years you germinated here,
Louisiana-rooted, marsh and hill —
From buckled bluffs the Red carves stark and sheer
To wetlands where the river has its will —

And as you grew you came to see and know
Moist meadow beauties, goat's-rue, greenbrier strung
By pinewood bogs, cold holly-oaks in snow,
And lyre-leaf sage whose song is never sung.

But now Sewanee's mountain is your home
Where other flowers surround you and you bloom
By rock and trail and hollow when you roam
On foot or bike or look out from your room:

The meadow rue and rue anemone,
A Carolina allspice picked for Joe,
The fall's grass-of-Parnassus left to me,
Forget-me-nots I'll scatter as you go

Down from the mountain to a world you bring
Seeds blossoming in each new fall and spring.

The Scholar

His mindful eyes take in the poem he reads
Again and yet again until it lives
Inside of him suspended while he gives
As gloss whatever help a student needs.

He knows in depth the author and his time,
The history of the text and of its form,
Alert to variations from the norm
In stanza, line, caesura, foot, and rhyme.

He works with grace, intent and yet serene,
Not twisting sense to serve a will to power
That pays off in the academic bower
But saying what the words most likely mean.

And so he writes brief notes with modest pride,
All pointing toward the poem they lie beside.

Headmaster, Mother, Son

A mother and the tired headmaster sat
Relaxing in his office while her son
Was being interviewed, but then their chat
Grew tense once her hard questions had begun.

The mother said, "Headmaster, let's be clear.
This prep school is elite and rigorous,
Expensive, too, so if our son comes here
What's in it in the end for him and us?

Will he succeed in business, politics,
Make good connections, have his name put down
Before some flashy whiz kid's from the sticks
For Princeton, Harvard, Yale, Cornell, or Brown?"

"Yes, Madam, if your boy is bright enough
To be admitted, works hard, he'll do well
Because our old curriculum is tough,
But that is not an end on which we dwell."

"Then what," quipped she, "is your primary goal?"
(Miffed and bewildered, letting out her breath);
And he, "To tend to body, mind, and soul
And to prepare him, in a word, for death."

Headmaster Leaving

The snowflakes on the oaks have stayed the same
Through all the changing winters of the years
As every boy's bright face has since I came
To make pressed lips articulate with tears.

The scrums, the prep-times, first loves, chapel prayers,
The Founders' Days, the war dead etched on brass,
Strict prefects calling *lights out* from the stairs —
These were the holy texts in memory's mass.

And though I bore the headship and its stress —
Hirings, firings, urging Old Boys to give
And give again, yet doing more with less,
My life a death through which a school might live —

This classroom was my own, oak-paneled, small,
Unfitted with those terminals and screens
New colleagues have to have all down the hall,
Their chalkboards not on walls but in machines.

And here each year a dwindling remnant read
That first and greatest tale of rage and lust,
Dreaming of Helen's breasts and Hector dead,
Troy's battlements collapsed in burning dust.

Yet now at last I leave this room for good
Where ghosts still whisper Greek attentively
While twilight blooms through panes in Gothic wood
And snow in oaks falls silent over me.

Two Poems on Quietude

1. Old Office, in Retirement

Five long hard years away
To be department chair
I'm back at last to stay
And breathe a calmer air,
No timelines to compel,
No problem personnel,

Reports, bad budget news,
Evaluations, pleas
For grades, tense interviews,
Administrationese
In which too much I've sung
And not the mother tongue.

And thus I'm here again
Where music, books, and tea,
Blank paper and this pen
Will be enough for me,
Familiars of a soul
By quietude made whole.

2. Familiars

They haunt these rooms and halls, their native place,
Attendants that will gather by the side
Of all come home for good to private space
Where inwardness and quietude abide.

A child's milk-bottle nipple split with age,
A confirmation Bible's tattered spine,
An old love-letter's fading yellow page,
A farewell poem that lacks its final line —

Such things dismissed as sentiment, cliché
Are guarded night and day by spirits blest,
Driving cool analytic mind away
From reminiscences the heart knows best,

Those images so luminous, discrete,
Connected till a life is made complete.

Peasant Girl Day-Dreaming

after the painting by Jean-François Millet (1814-1875)
1848
oil on panel

1

The distaff on her lap, the spindle dangling
Between her knees from a limp left arm,
The fingers all but ready to let go,
She cools bare feet on earth still undisturbed.

This is her special place to think and dream,
A settled talus boulder for her seat,
A wall of rocks moldering though it holds
The steady weight of elbow, hand, and chin.

Twin trees behind her long have taken root,
Their branches interweaving as they rise
Above green seedlings that can only grow
Stunted between the canopy and ground.

The woman is a shepherdess, her flock
Grazing somewhere nearby yet out of sight.
Her gaze is toward the one she would become.
The woolen threads she'll spin tell what she is.

Beyond the rocks, against a slate blue sky
A sun, pale as the clouds, is almost gone
Leaving behind a face still lost in light,
Not solar, but the dream-like light of dreams.

And there she stays, both other and the same,
Suspended in a soft and fluid glow,
Floating past resignation and regret
Toward husband, children, Paris, riches, fame

Then back, a warp and woof of fancy, fact,
No willowy figure with a low-cut blouse
Tight-corseted but a sturdy girl whose dress
Is loosely fitted, flowing like a robe.

2

Her world is not Watteau's nor yet Millet's
Where gleaners gather up the fatal grain
But one in which her yearning still belongs
With distaff, spindle, sheepdog, staff, and sheep.

Her pensive sadness holds her, holds Millet,
Far from the clash of citizen and king,
The masses, troops, and bloody barricades,
That Paris he had fled for Barbizon.

And there, in fear, ill health, and poverty —
Rheumatic pain migrating joint to joint —
He came home to a place he'd never seen,
Painting a light whose source is not the sun

But cheeks that bloom as the smooth brushstrokes dry
On panel made of heartwood by a man
Who like the girl through dreams could wander free
Or flower in the ruins of Arcady.

As Far As Light Remains

All alone in twilight a cold crow is calling
Out of the leafless tree while near and far away
As far as light remains a ghostly snow is falling.

So, when dying thinkers over-vexed with galling
Enigmas of the mind cry out for one more day
All alone in twilight a cold crow is calling.

And the poets, lost in dream, wordlessly recalling
Images of Eden find that words can only say
As far as light remains a ghostly snow is falling.

Even theologians who strain to hear enthralling
Yet silent choirs of angels fear that every day
All alone in twilight a cold crow is calling.

Physicists, too, who'd think it too appalling
If Love were our First Cause are simply left to say
As far as light remains a ghostly snow is falling.

Yet where these others falter, silent lovers sprawling
In love's sweet after-sadness say best in their own way
All alone in twilight a cold crow is calling
As far as light remains a ghostly snow is falling.

On Recovering the Use of His Eyes

after the Latin verse of Samuel Johnson (1709-1784)

Universal Lord, who tempers the rife
Vicissitudes of everything in life,
Who bids the night, gloomy in icy cold,
Be changed into the limpid morning gold,
Who willed it that, by humid clouds obscured,
Puffed up by stinging blood, my eyes be cured:
Where pleasing day but heightened my dark fright
You brought me health and gave me back to light.
Lord, how can I attend in prayer and praise?
A student of the Bible all my days,
O may I ever, rightly, in my station,
Honor you with useful application:
For, Father, proper thanks to you are given
By him who uses well the gifts of heaven.

Wells

In Norse legend, Odin had to tear out and sacrifice his right eye in exchange for a drink from Mimir's well — The Well of Wisdom. The waters of this well held the knowledge not only of what things were but why things had to be. Mimir took Odin's eye and threw it into the well where it is said to shine forever.

A round wall made of native clay and lime
Put up to stop a dreamer just in time
Or warn a king thirsty for something more
Than water from the well's deep flowing floor.

Beside the wall, a statue — lichened, worn —
Its head struck off, a green man long foresworn
Or Mimir, Odin's "wise rememberer,"
Who knew not only what but why things were . . .

One polished coin was all I had to show,
Its head an Indian chief, tail, buffalo,
So with a wish I flipped it in the well
But whether heads came up I could not tell

And my wish thus be granted for the ground
Under the spring that fed the well, though sound,
Rose from a place where shadows go before
And after things that gleam then gleam no more.

Yet, heads or tails, my wish might still come true
For none know how and why some wishes do
Once made upon whatever What or Who
May be in wells we peer at now, not through.

The ravens on the crank-rope, bucket lip,
Drinking from rain and well-spring, drop and sip,
The green man's body splotched with yellow-green,
His brow above the grass, his face unseen:

Are such things surfaces that nothing delves,
Literal symbols given to themselves,
Or were they, at the core, as good as one
Till *is* first twined with *like* and came undone?

All things are wells. A Digger dug them, left,
And left us under-diggers in the cleft
Where, that long noon, still shoveling at the base,
We saw, through welling dark, the stars in place.

Then climbing step by step we heard, below,
Groundwater swelling, quickening its flow
Both from and toward a fountain at the source,
Time out of mind in time its only course.

There, coins, like wishing stars, still twinkle, fall,
But whether calling heads has helped at all
And which side faces up we no more know
Than water's mirroring windows blindly show.

Yet at a depth we once could reach and mark
A Sioux's head and a bison lie in dark
Not far from Odin's eye, the price of sight,
Reflecting in the unreflected light.

Shepherdess and Flock at Sunset

after the picture by Jean-François Millet (1814-1875)
ca. 1868-1870
pastel and black conté crayon on wove paper

He loved the twilight dimming into dusk
Through which a peasant walked his donkey on
From long days pitching wheat in summer fields,
No Joseph going home to Bethlehem . . .

But here, for once, a blinding sunset bursts
So bright the sun itself is lost in light
Whose white core sets the lower air aflame
And spreads along a thread of plain and sky.

The plain is featureless, no crumbled wall
Or tower's rubble-stone, just grass and gorse
Where sheep as brown as earth nibble the ground
And one small boulder where a shepherdess

Sits knitting with her back against the blaze,
Weaving her destined threads while sinking rays
That soon will flare at dusk to die in night
Still faintly paint a sky with Mary's blue.

Vigils

a North Louisianian looks south

January 6, Epiphany and the first day of Mardi Gras

The quiet alone is holy and enough
So long as night still darkens into dawn
And fallen starlight rises from a lawn
Whose snowflakes twinkle deep in matter's stuff.

And on this night when hope and fear grew calm
The Wise Men knelt where Child and Mother were
With gifts of gold and frankincense and myrrh
For king and god, for soul and body's balm.

And as the words of Matthew draw me in
Once more to where the heart and mind are one
Though history and myth have come undone
In these late days when faith itself is sin

I think how many winters just the same
Revels of music, food, drink, dance, and sex
Have ruled with Orpheus, Comus, Bacchus, Rex —
Those passing kings great crowds loudly acclaim.

Now stars of Hollywood outshine the Star
With glittering gifts all wise men would disdain
Though thousands wait for throws in dark and rain,
Not Gaspar, Melchior, and Balthazar.

And so Old Adam still will have his day
As celebrant at feasts some people keep
For flesh and blood that never wake from sleep,
This bread and wine of human show and play.

Yet now and then forever in the fields
Of space and time whose carnivals will end
Shepherds abide through night to watch and tend
Till Wise Men come to know and knowledge yields.

The Break-In

How strange seeing your poems in a book . . .
I once could feel the pathos of those nights
About them still in hottest Baton Rouge,
Black coffee, poverty, the sweated line!
 — John Finlay (1941-1991),
 "To a Friend on His First Book,"
 Between the Gulfs (1986)

Some forty years ago . . . yet in my mind
From time to time I see those rooms again —
That spare unshared apartment where you lived,
Earning the Ph.D. at LSU —
A bed half-made, a nightstand with its lamp,
Ash tray, and cigarettes, and on the floor
A stack of books you read, then underscored,
Engaging every text, intently fixed,
Your very being seemingly at stake,
Choragos in tense dialogue with kings,
From Holy Writ and Plato's Socrates
To Thomas, Dante, and the troubled reigns
Of Nietzsche, Freud, Tate, Kafka, Winters, James,
All actors in the drama of a soul
You strove to save from tragic turn and fall.

Your place had little more — a single pan
To heat up coffee-water on the stove,
A black typewriter with its sticky keys,
Long yellow pads for drafts of verse and prose,
Scenes from your struggles with the Gnostic gods
Then foreign to an Alabama farm
Whose seasons of the church and earth were one.

And there you'd dwelt among the things that tell —
Spring dogwoods, Easter lilies, hyacinths,

Late summer's morning glories, white and blue,
The fall's frost-aster petals on the ground,
And Christmas holly weaving winter peace
For mantel, yard, grave, chancel, garden, door,
Or pastures you would cross to reach a slope
With sisters watching as you called and traced
Between the primum mobile and pond
The northern constellations, name by name —
The Hunter and the Dragon and the Lyre —
Job's Coffin held aloft by dark and stars.

Sometimes that realm could seem so far away
And yet be near "in hottest Baton Rouge"
Where you walked back one night to quiet rooms
From wine and conversation, new work shared
Through dinner with likeminded poet friends
To spy a door ajar, a window prized
By thieves who'd broken in but then had found
Nothing worth stealing — old clothes, older books,
A manual Underwood, fair-copies typed,
Ashes of finished cigarettes and thoughts,
No TV, radio, hi-fi, or cash —
And so fled empty-handed, cursing God.

And when you saw that all you had was there —
The cinder-block bookshelves' unpainted boards
Still holding Shakespeare, Milton undisturbed —
A poor man dancing past the robber band,
You knew you had been faithful to a gift
The Holy Ghost as Muse bestowed at birth,
Plowing by mind and hand down lines and rows,
True to the ancient sanctions of the land.

And though in your own way you'd come to drink
Like Socrates the poison of the age —

Narcissus leaning breathless to the pool,
Sherlock aroused for Moriarty's kiss —
You wrote late poems and essays to be whole,
Returning to that place where you were born,
Full harvests of a Blood Moon in the fields
As you stayed up all night, suffering AIDS
A decade while completing those two books,
Your story left for others who would strive
For mind's integrity, which, years ago,
A break-in had confirmed, exemplified,
As did your final moment's final breath
When from your deathbed halfway rising up,
With blinded eyes you looked beyond and said
"Plato?" to one now sent to take you home
To that last, great symposium of Love
At which the conversation never ends.

The Striking of the Lyre
Demodokos in Modernity
A Statement on Poetics

When, in *The Odyssey*, we first behold Odysseus, he is weeping on the shore of Kalypso's isle, gazing over the waves toward Penelope and home and thus toward his intended human place and fate — not as divine consort to a goddess nor yet as a shade in Hades, nor as one of Circe's herd — but as ruler of far-off Ithaca, an island realm in the middle world washed by the middle sea.

But then, set free by the will of Zeus, Odysseus, with Kalypso's own strong olive-handled ax, fashions a raft out of the felled black poplar and alder trunks, a raft that takes him over the turbulent waters until it breaks apart — and floating for two long days upon a single beam, at last from atop a rising wave he has an "unexpected glimpse of wooded land" and then is swept away onto the rocky shores of remote Phaiakia to whose untroubled people the gods still show themselves without disguise.

Guarding his identity, Odysseus comes as a nameless stranger to the palace of Alkinoos near which lie perfect gardens with their "orderly / rows of greens, all kinds . . . lush through the seasons" and orchards of pomegranates, apples, figs, and pears whose fruit is exhausted or spoiled "neither in winter time nor summer." And in this pastoral kingdom, Odysseus hears the bard Demodokos sing twice to his fine "clear lyre" of Odysseus' own role in the Trojan War, including the final ruse of the wooden horse.

In response to the powerful singing, this "stranger" — whose own great exploits have been thus traumatically revealed in the rhythms and in the words of measured verse — first seeks privacy by hiding his head under his purple mantle, yet then uncovers, and, by pure compulsion, publicly weeps: "tears running down his face before the Phaiakians." And when Demodokos pauses, Odysseus — who soon after such singing will at last risk revealing his identity to his host — once again "would take the mantle away from his head, and wipe the tears off, / and taking up a two-handed goblet would pour a libation to the gods." And so this crafty hero, who wept for the return to his full humanity on the sands of Kalypso's isle, now weeps from the depths of his being at poetry's shattering revelation of who he is.

This profound effect of poetry on a hero both modern and archaic is among the most compelling evidence we have that our greatest verse and the mystery of human existence are at one. And there are other clues. Keats, for instance, in his search for ideal disinterestedness, named Socrates and Jesus as the only persons in history who attained to such a state, though their teachings were taken down — perhaps in necessary accordance with this ideal — only by others. Yet what do we find when we examine the final acts of these two figures who so readily stand as symbols of the two great strains in the Western tradition — the Greco-Roman and the Judeo-Christian?

Awaiting death in his cell, Socrates turned Aesop's *Fables* and the *Prelude to Apollo* into verse because his daimon had said for him to "practice and cultivate the arts," and fearing now that not philosophy but poiesis was intended, Socrates says: "I thought it would be safer not to take my departure before I had cleared my conscience by writing poetry and so obeying the dream." Likewise, on the cross, before the final cry that escapes him with his spirit, Christ, according to Matthew, utters his last words in the poetry of the Psalms: ("*Eli, Eli, lama sabachthani?*" Psalm 22:1). Even Plato, whose life and thought link Socrates and Jesus, declared on his deathbed, by the slightest gesture, the *differentia specifica* of verse: "Plato died at the age of eighty-one. On the evening of his death he had a Thracian girl play the flute to him. The girl could not find the beat of the *nomos*. With a movement of his finger, Plato indicated to her the Measure" (Eric Voegelin).

The origin of measured verse is lost in prehistory. But it seems reasonable to suppose that, in some long defining moment, primitive man awoke from animal sleep and so was struck with wonder and with terror at the beauty and the mystery of a world in which he seemed fated to dwell as a being on the verge, placed in a middle station somewhere above the flora and the fauna and the elements, yet well below divine powers obscurely apprehended. The cycling of the seasons, the progress of the stars, the rhythms of the body and the stages of human life — such things must have drawn forth from out of the depths a first measured response to consciousness both in music and in words. Perhaps at last man recognized a strange power in language that led him to think of the Maker's power as a language in itself, an attribute of deity, as in the Book of Genesis, where, in God's own mind, the *word* "light" somehow came before and helped to give existence to the *thing* called "light": "And God *said*, 'Let there be light'; and there *was* light" (Genesis 1:3).

The story of Adam the Namer, who spoke to the answering beasts before the Fall, and the story of the Fall itself as involving disruption — not only between human beings and the other creatures and between language and things but even between words and the very Word itself — may be archaic indicators that poetry lies at the center of human life and remains the one power by which man might still return from his long sojourn through history to a realm where Edenic innocence and conscious existence, both in time and beyond time, are reconciled at last.

Such reconciliation may be symbolized by Homer's bard Demodokos, who sang of the fall of Troy amid the gardens and the orchards of Alkinoos' pastoral kingdom. And indeed, it is King Alkinoos himself, who, in one of the most remarkable passages in *The Odyssey*, encourages Odysseus, so profoundly stirred by Demodokos' song, to transform himself from listener into poet not only to tell his own story but also to say why he weeps at tragic history, for such history, says the king, is not the final end but rather a godly gift for a further, sublime purpose: "Explain to us also what secret sorrow makes you weep as you listen to the tragic story of the Argives and the fall of Troy. Were not the gods responsible for that, weaving catastrophe into the pattern of events to make a song for future generations?"

And to this may we not add that as long as human beings continue to ask those two primary philosophical questions — Why is there a universe instead of nothing and Why is that universe as it is and not otherwise? — poets will try to write what Wallace Stevens called the "central poem," a poem in which the poet attempts the great return from the fallen world to the Bible's *peaceable kingdom* (Isaiah 11: 1-9). Such poets will glimpse what Jacques Maritain calls "the radiance of the ontological mystery," and, like Caedmon, the cowherd poet and symbolic initiator of the English poetic tradition, they will "Sing about the Creation." And should the authors of these poems ever close the circle of being — if such an act be possible and allowed — then, like Adam the Namer, they and we may commune once more with all those things which, even now, as the Psalmist says, mysteriously converse among themselves: "Day to day pours forth speech, and night to night declares knowledge . . . There is no speech . . . yet their voice goes out through all the earth and their words to the end of the world" (Psalm 19: 2-4).

To all such poets who attempt the "central poem" should go the praise Odysseus himself bestows upon the Phaiakian: "No one on earth can help honoring and respecting the bards, for the Muse has taught them the art of song and she loves the minstrel fraternity." So the doer of great deeds pays homage to one of those through whom such deeds live on, Demodokos, whose measured verse was chanted to the striking of the lyre.

— David Middleton

The Author

Until his retirement in June of 2010, David Middleton served for thirty-three years as Professor of English, Poet-in-Residence, Distinguished Service Professor, Alcee Fortier Distinguished Professor, and Head of the Department of Languages and Literature at Nicholls State University in Thibodaux, Louisiana. In August of 2014, he was named the first Poet in Residence Emeritus at Nicholls.

Middleton's books of verse include *The Burning Fields* (LSU Press, 1991), *As Far As Light Remains* (The Cummington Press [Harry Duncan], 1993), *Beyond the Chandeleurs* (LSU Press, 1999), *The Habitual Peacefulness of Gruchy: Poems After Pictures by Jean-François Millet* (LSU Press, 2005), and *The Fiddler of Driskill Hill: Poems* (LSU Press, 2013).

Middleton has also published several chapbooks of verse including *The Language of the Heart* (Louisiana Literature Press, 2003), which was cited by *The Advocate* (Baton Rouge) as the best book of verse by a Louisianian for 2003.

In March of 2014, *The Fiddler of Driskill Hill* won Second Honorable Mention from the Louisiana Library Association as Best Book of the Year for 2013 by a Louisianian or about Louisiana.

In April of 2006, Middleton won The Allen Tate Award for best verse published in *The Sewanee Review* in 2005. In November of 2006, Middleton received the State of Louisiana Governor's Award for Outstanding Professional Artist of 2006. In October of 2022, Middleton was the featured poet in the annual "A Night of Poetry With . . ." series in New York City, sponsored by *First Things*.

Middleton has served for over thirty years as literary executor for Alabama poet and essayist John Martin Finlay (1941-1991). Middleton was the editor, along with John P. Doucet, of a comprehensive, annotated, two-volume edition of Finlay's poetry and prose: *"Dense Poems & Socratic Light": The Poetry of John Martin Finlay (1941–1991)* and *"With Constant Light": The Collected Essays and Reviews, with Selections from the Diaries, Letters, and Other Prose of John Martin Finlay (1941–1991)*. These volumes were published in the summer of 2020 by Wiseblood Books.

Printed in the USA
CPSIA information can be obtained
at www.ICGtesting.com
LVHW041743131223
766027LV00031B/704/J